L8061

AMERICA AND ASIA

AMERICA AND ASIA

Problems of Today's War and
the Peace of Tomorrow

by

OWEN LATTIMORE

&

Foreword by
Admiral H. E. Yarnell, U.S.N., Retired

CLAREMONT, CALIFORNIA

1943

PUBLISHED BY CLAREMONT COLLEGES

CLAREMONT, CALIFORNIA, FOR

THE THREE ASSOCIATED COLLEGES AT CLAREMONT

POMONA COLLEGE

SCRIPPS COLLEGE

CLAREMONT COLLEGES

Copyright 1943
Claremont Colleges, Claremont, California

FOREWORD

IN MY school-boy days, we studied a textbook entitled: "Outlines of World History." This volume dealt with the ancient civilizations of the near East and Europe, but there was not a single reference to China, Japan, or the Far East. It is no wonder that there has been, and is now in the West, an amazing ignorance of the history of the nations in this area which has become so dominant in this war.

To those who follow the course of the war, it is becoming evident that China has been fighting the battles of the western democracies for six years.

The defeat of Japan hinges largely on the support given China in her desperate struggle.

The war in the West and the East are one and the same war. To quote the lecturer—"The end of this war can more quickly be brought about by the allies acting together and considering the Western theatre and the Eastern and Pacific theatres as theatres of a common war to be directed in common and not in order of priority."

It is also being realized that there can be no peace in the world unless there is peace in the Far East and this depends on the emergence of China as a strong and stable nation. We need have no fear that China will ever embark on a policy of world conquest. Her philosophy throughout the ages has been against such procedure.

There is no one better qualified to interpret the Far East to our people than Mr. Owen Lattimore. For many years, at first hand, by travel and by study, he has familiarized himself with the past history and the present problems of China and other nations of this area.

The Claremont Colleges and the sponsors of this lecture course are filling a vital need in making available to the public the knowledge, wisdom and experience of outstanding authorities on world topics.

Never in our history has such knowledge and understanding been so necessary as at the present time. If the framers of the treaties that follow this war are guided by such men, there is hope that the world may have peace for many generations.

H. E. YARNELL

May 31, 1943   Admiral, U.S.N., Retired.

CONTENTS

AMERICA'S PART IN THE
PACIFIC WAR

I.

AMERICA'S PART IN THE
PACIFIC WAR

O<small>UR</small> generation of Americans has just had a unique opportunity to advance its understanding of problems on the other side of the Pacific. Madame Chiang's visit to this country has focused for us not only the drama but the importance of our allied country, China, across the Pacific; but there is something that even Madame Chiang cannot do for us and that is to develop our own knowledge of the facts and our own understanding of what those facts mean.

As individuals and as a people we must understand these things for ourselves. We need to understand why we are in this war, how we got into this war, how we are fighting it and what is to come of it. When we examine our own record in the understanding of political events and political responsibilities, the outstanding fact that confronts us is that we, who have always considered ourselves the leading democracy of the world, have been behind the Chinese in correctly analyzing the processes of the world in which we live. We have been accustomed to think of the Far East as an area in which we had certain interests, and in which we could intervene if we liked. We did not understand that the Far East in this twentieth century has come so close to us that, in a sense, we are in it whether we want to be or not. Our failure to understand this resulted in our being knocked into this war by a treacherous attack after we ourselves had failed either to prevent the war or to evade it.

In short, the fact that we are in this war at all is a serious criticism of the political common sense of the whole American people. It is a serious criticism because we could, with the help of other nations, have stopped it before it began—long before Pearl Harbor overtook us. We could have stopped it in Manchuria in 1931. We could have stopped it in Abyssinia, in Spain, in Czechoslovakia. We did not stop it, and it overtook us.

We are accustomed to think of ourselves as a most progressive and enlightened people—the model democracy of our time. We ought to consider what kind of responsibility that lays upon us. We have the most free and the most well-informed press and radio in the world. Throughout the years leading up to Pearl Harbor, every American could buy a paper and turn on his radio and get the latest information from all over the world. This was provided for him by highly

paid experts using an enormously expensive, complicated network which gathered facts and provided
information in a matter of hours or even minutes.
Moreover, if an American wanted to get not only
the news but a political interpretation of the news, he
was free to choose whatever paper he wanted to buy
according to its editorial policy. He could read the
columnists and listen over the radio to the commentators that he himself preferred. If any people in the
world ought to have known what kind of world we
have been living in and what to do about it, it was
the American people, and we failed. Pearl Harbor
caught us flat-footed.

I think we ought to examine our own consciences
and admit that the defeat of Pearl Harbor cannot be
written off just by blaming the people who were
caught flat-footed on the spot, because the whole nation was caught flat-footed. The shock of Pearl Harbor awakened us to the fact that we are not living in
the kind of world we had thought we were living in. In
spite of our freedom of information, our freedom to
discuss facts, our freedom to decide what to do about
it, we had arrived at the conclusion that we were living in one kind of a world when, in fact, we were living in a quite different kind of world. And it is my
belief that disasters like Pearl Harbor do not happen

to people who know what kind of world they are living in.

Nor can we, because after all we are a democratic people, evade the responsibility by blaming the Administration or the State Department, or the Army and Navy. The responsibility falls on us, the whole people. We had all the individual facts that could have enabled us to understand what kind of menace, what kind of war, was hanging over us. It was we, the people, who refused to fit those facts together and come to a decision. The President, as early as 1938, called on us to quarantine the aggressor. We were not ready to go along with him. The Navy called for the fortification of Guam. We, the people, refused either to vote the money for the fortifications or to adopt a policy of joint action with other nations which would have made the fortifications unnecessary. In a democracy, responsibilities of this kind always come back straight to the people, the whole people.

I think it would do us good to compare ourselves in this respect with the Chinese. We are accustomed to think of the Chinese as being, compared with us, a backward people. There are at least a couple of hundred million Chinese who are totally illiterate. There are at least a couple of hundred million people in

China who have never ridden in a motor vehicle. There are many, many millions who have never even seen a train. There are relatively few newspapers in China and, relatively speaking, there is only a handful of people who have radios of their own. Yet the Chinese, with all these handicaps, did know and did understand the kind of world they were living in. They knew what they were going to have to face well before the Marco Polo Bridge incident of 1937 and they walked up open-eyed and faced it. They faced it not only with courage but with a solid unity that astonished the whole world.

We in America are still inclined to think of this war as something that sneaked up on us. We think of it as starting from a small beginning in Asia and spreading insidiously to Abyssinia, Spain and Czechoslovakia until it crept up on us and we found ourselves overwhelmed with a war of world dimensions. This is precisely where the Chinese were ahead of us; not in knowledge, but in political intelligence and political maturity. They understood years before we did that every step of the developments leading to the war, every decision faced, every decision evaded, was not a local question. For at least a quarter of a century there has not in fact been what our pundits and wiseacres and commentators were so ready to describe as "the Far Eastern question" or "the Sino-Japanese crisis." The Chinese knew, as we did not, that every crisis and problem involved was in reality only a local or Far Eastern aspect of questions of world scope and world scale.

This is an assertion that can be documented from speeches and writings by Generalissimo Chiang Kai-shek and many other Chinese leaders over a long term of years. Moreover, behind the generation of Generalissimo Chiang Kai-shek there stands one of the greatest figures in modern history, still far too little understood in this country—Sun Yat-sen, who throughout the revolutionary career in which he created the spirit of modern China, never tired of trying to persuade the western nations and the world as a whole to understand China and the Far East, not as something distant, recondite, mysterious, difficult to understand, something to be shut up in a far-away geographical compartment, but something which was a part of the structure of the politics and the economy of the whole world.

The Chinese of our generation did make one mistake. When the Japanese attacked them at Mukden, in 1931, ten years before Pearl Harbor, the Chinese tried to negotiate instead of fighting. Their mistake was that they thought that in the League of Nations there was a system that would be strong enough to take care of such international banditry. They did not believe that the great powers could be politically so stupid as to throw the door wide open to the imperialist aggression of Japan. After that the Chinese made no more mistakes. They knew they would have to fight, and they knew they would have to begin fighting alone. We in this country are far from appreciating as yet the coolness and the courage with which the Chinese walked into what was then a very dark future. I was there at the time and I saw it.

What kept the Chinese going, before they had allies? One important factor in their resistance was the realization that they were fighting not simply for national survival, and certainly for no selfish advantage, but for issues that affected every people in the world. If China defended these issues, then Japanese aggression would gradually force the same issues on every other people in the world. Eventually the other peoples would no longer be able to hide their heads in the sand and pretend that they were avoiding these issues. Gradually, all those who were in danger would be forced over to one side, the same side as the Chinese, and eventually all the aggressors would line up on the other side. What the great powers refused to understand by the exercise of their own intelligence, they would be forced to deal with by the rapacity of the aggressors whom they were then trying to appease.

What made the Chinese right in their judgment was their grasp of a very simple principle, and I wish that a similar understanding of that principle were to be found in everyday discussion here in this country. This is the principle that democracy, whether we define it as liberty, equality, and fraternity, or as the right to vote, or the right to work out solutions by discussion and adjustment in order to assure the greatest good for the greatest number, is not a fixed system. Democracy, however else you define it, is not static, is not a fixed system; and this principle of politics and history the Chinese people of today understand.

Democracy, in working practice, is a way of doing things that must either get better and better or get worse and worse. It never stays the same. If it gets better, it can only get better by being made available to more and more people all the time. If it gets worse, then very rapidly it gets to a stage at which there are so few people enjoying the privileges of democracy that the actual privileges of the few count more than the nominal rights of the many. When a democracy gets to that stage, it is likely to turn suddenly into something else; facism, imperialism, or some other system of legalized inequality and codified undemocraticness.

Of course, the Chinese had reasons for being more sharply awake to these questions than we ourselves. They had been struggling for a hundred years, first to prevent their country from being divided up by a number of hungry powers, then to try to reform the decaying Manchu dynasty. Then, when they despaired of reform, they tried to overthrow that dynasty and substitute a Chinese Republic; and after that they had still to win equality for their nation among other nations.

It was at this point that a clash between China and Japan became inevitable. The progress of the Chinese toward equality in their own country had got to the point where it challenged the imperialistic privileges of other countries. Several of these countries were tenacious enough of their privileges; but the Japanese were not only tenacious—they were bent on extending their privileges and increasing their control over China's territory and the life of the Chinese people. The issue was one that could not be avoided. The Chinese had either to go forward or go back. They refused to go back; and the Japanese were determined to try to push them back by force.

During this period we in this country were badly confused by our failure to understand that China could not be a progressive country simply in verbal terms; that if the Chinese were to be progressive they had to get something out of it. We allowed ourselves to be badly shaken by the Japanese propaganda that the Chinese were an unruly people incapable of running their own country, of "setting their own house in order," as the celebrated saying went. We were inclined to let pass or to believe the Japanese tale that the Japanese themselves were not unruly; that the Japanese were a dynamic people; that they had a destiny to rule the unruly millions of Asia. We totally failed to see that Japan's aggression did not spring from being a "have not" nation. The Japanese never were a "have not" nation. They never were nearly as much a "have not" nation as a peaceful and orderly country like Sweden today. The Japanese were a "have not" nation only in one sense; that they could not, out of the resources of their own country, build up and maintain a navy and army and air force of a size that could only be used for aggressive purposes. They were a "have not" nation because they demanded the right to get from other countries the raw materials to set going their own aggression against those very countries.

In Japan, just as in Germany, the springs of aggression were not within the race, but within the social order. The Japanese had strong survivals of a feudal system of codified inequalities between social classes. The privileged people who benefited by the system refused to abolish it, because of the inconveniences it would have caused them. As an alternative, they launched into aggression in order to force other people to pay the price of keeping up the expensive and inefficient social system within Japan.

Once the war began it became immediately, for the Chinese, a war which involved the necessity for going ahead in a democratic direction. The Chinese had just come within sight, under the Generalissimo's leadership, of a full unity which gave the Central Government control and power in every corner of the country. They were just coming within reach of the ability to manage their economic life on a national scale. They had come near to ridding themselves of the curse of civil war and warlordism, things which had always been fostered by the system of unequal treaties and had been deliberately fomented by the way in which the Japanese used those unequal treaties to harbor, under the Japanese flag in Japanese concessions, all the political scallywags in China. It was because the Chinese were on the edge of the rewards of the revolution which Sun Yat-sen had started and which the Generalissimo had been fulfilling that the Japanese struck, in order to prevent peace and order and civilized modes of development in China.

It is difficult to describe the democracy of China in terms that fit the ordinary American textbook. The Chinese are a people who have had for many centuries a great deal of democratic practice in their social life, in the relation of man to man and of group to group within society; but they have not had the political system of legally defined and guaranteed rights which the Western world has called democracy since the nineteenth century. The Chinese have, however, now come to the point where they are prepared to combine the best of what is socially democratic in their own heritage and tradition with the essential political standards common to all modern democratic peoples. That is one reason why they have been able to fight so well—because they have been fighting not only to stay alive but to get something that makes life worth living in a deeper and nobler sense. Out of the very fact that they have fought so long there developed something which Americans do not as yet, I think, fully understand. To put it concisely, the war which broke out in Europe in 1939 and the war in which America became involved after Pearl Harbor were largely predetermined in the forms which they have taken by the fact that the Chinese had been fighting first and fighting for so long. The Chinese, by preventing successful aggression, turned the aggressors in other directions. By so doing, they also sharpened the demands of the aggressors for a kind of domination that could not be satisfied by even the most persistent and obstinate appeasers in the western democracies. To put it in another and historically very significant way: The Chinese, by fighting for a democracy which they did not yet have, forced other countries to fight for the democracy which they had inherited from their ancestors.

However, there is also another aspect. We have long fallen into the way of giving an almost tolerant and condescending tone to our praise of Chinese courage and Chinese resistance. We talk about how the Chinese have stood up to superior Japanese armaments (largely made out of American metals) with only their own flesh and blood. We have failed to realize that the Chinese have also fought a very brainy and very skillful war. It is perhaps a shock when you first realize this. Of the four major united nations of the present day only two have withstood the Axis on a large scale on wide land fronts. Those two are Russia and China, which we had always considered inferior to ourselves in efficiency and technical skill. The Japanese rolled us and the British back from the Philippines, Hong Kong, Malaya, and Burma, and the Dutch from Netherlands India, with shocking speed. Even the Dutch, who are by European standards a small and weak nation, had in Netherlands India better modern equipment, and more of it, than the Chinese had when they began fighting in 1937. If we compare our defeats with the way in which the Chinese have constantly kept the war going on the main Japanese fronts, and behind the Japanese fronts in what are called, not very accurately, the occupied territories, we are forced to realize that war is not only a question of superior manufacturing ability and superior weight of equipment; it is a question also of the intelligence with which equipment is used.

We Americans are rather slow at getting into war. When we have been really aroused by the demands of war I do not think that anybody fights more stubbornly or more skillfully than we do. But until we have got to that point in this war we must acknowledge that the Chinese have been more skillful soldiers than we have been.

Immediately after the Japanese attacked North China at the Marco Polo bridge, the Chinese forced them to attack Shanghai in the Yangtze valley. In so doing the Chinese scored their first strategic victory. They forced the Japanese to fight on fronts that covered the whole of China, when the Japanese plan had been to carry out a piece-by-piece war, isolating a few provinces at a time. The Chinese fought delaying actions across the breadth of the great eastern plains, always avoiding a Tannenberg encirclement, always avoiding the annihilation of their best trained forces, always keeping their armies intact. They drew the Japanese on. At times they lashed back. Tomorrow (April 7) is the anniversary of the Battle of Taierh-chuang, in which the Chinese inflicted crippling losses on two of the crack armored divisions of Japan. This victory is important not only in the history of the war in China but in the history of modern war, because here the Chinese, considered to be an unequipped, unmodern, unskillful army, actually for the first time showed how to throw a blitzkrieg for a loss, how to take on an enemy of superior equipment, extend him, maneuver him into the position you want, cut him off, smother the spearheads and blot out the superior armored divisions. For this aspect of the battle of Taierhchuang the Chinese have never yet had sufficient credit.

The Chinese eventually fell back to the line which has been more or less permanent since the fall of Han-

kow and Canton at the end of 1938. It is a line based
on the most skillful use of terrain. Out in the open
flat plains of the east the Chinese cannot face the Japanese today because there the Japanese have the advantage of mechanized equipment, fast movement,
and quick concentration. From the air they can anticipate and stop Chinese concentrations, destroying
them with long-range artillery fire and with tanks at
shorter range. The Chinese counter the Japanese
tactics, which are based on superior materiel, by en-
gaging in light actions at the edges of the plains, draw-
ing the Japanese into more broken, hilly country and
there gradually splitting up the Japanese columns,
forcing them to follow the Chinese in smaller and
smaller groups. The Chinese then close in on these
groups like a tide and wear away at them with the light
armament which is practically all that they possess:
trench mortars, rifles, machine guns, hand grenades
and finally the bayonet. By the use of these tactics
the Chinese have been able to break up and drive back
every major Japanese offensive since 1939.

When the Chinese lost their seacoast they carried
out, parallel to their adoption of a new style of fighting, something that would have been a remarkable
achievement for any nation with the highest mechanical equipment. They made the Burma Road. I

must have read more thousands of words about the
Burma Road than most Americans and I do not think
I have yet seen it adequately explained that the Burma
Road was not a lifeline *into* China. It was a way *out* of
China made by the Chinese themselves. The significance of this lies in the fact that for a hundred years
the main process in the relations between China and
other countries had been the penetration of those other
countries into China. This time it was the Chinese who
broke out of their own country and broke a new gateway to the outer world. They did it by the most
fantastic and unbelievable application of human labor.
They did it when American and British engineers said
it couldn't be done, and they did it in a shorter time
than they themselves had said would be necessary;
and finally, when the Burma Road was lost, it was not
lost by the Chinese, but by China's allies.

The pride of the Chinese in the achievement of the
Burma Road is a psychological as well as a physical
factor in the mounting pressure on China since the
loss of the Burma Road. The engineering of the
Burma Road had been part of a complex Chinese cal-
culation. They had assumed that if they held on long
enough, fighting alone against Japan, they would
eventually get allies. They believed that the peoples
who would not willingly become their allies would in

time be forced to defend themselves against aggression, and so would necessarily become allies of China. This was what happened, but the Chinese did not anticipate, any more than we did, the rapidity and the enormous geographical sweep of the Japanese victories against America, Britain and Netherlands India.

Today the Chinese are still fighting a brainy and technically skillful war with steadily diminishing supplies. I am not a military expert, and what I might have to say to you about the relative importance of the Pacific theatre of war, or the question of Hitler first or Japan first, would not have any special value. But I can say to you something about the common stock of opinion in China on these matters. The proper starting point, I think, goes back to something that I have already touched on; namely, the Chinese feeling that when war was forced on them to begin with it was a world question and not a local question. I think the average Chinese feels today that winning this war is not a question of Hitler first or Japan first. The end of this war can more quickly be brought about by the allies acting together and considering the western theatres and the eastern and Pacific theatres as theatres of a common war to be directed in common and not in order of priority. Or rather, to put it still more clearly: certain priorities of action may be unavoidable, but these should not be allowed to lead to priorities of importance in the European and Asiatic *results* of the war.

Certainly the Chinese are no less willing than they were before to continue bearing more than their share of sacrifice. If you look back over the record you will find that one of the remarkable things about the Generalissimo's appeals to his people at the hours of recurrent crisis when the situation has been especially desperate in China is that he does not appeal primarily to the selfish interests of the Chinese alone. He always appeals to their highest interest and to their consciousness of being members of a world community. It is a remarkable thing, and I think an encouraging thing to anybody who believes in democracy, that the higher the appeal you make to the common people, the less you talk down to them, the more you appeal to them on a plane of nobility and unselfishness and generosity —the more magnificent the response you get. The Generalissimo has certainly proved that in China.

There is, however, another aspect to the purely military question of the war in the Pacific at the present time: although the first crushing and decisive victories at the end of this war may be won against Hitler, the major consequences of victory, the major issues to be settled, the major problems to be decided, may well be in Asia and the Pacific.

Part of the world of illusion that we have been living in ever since the last war is the illusion that democracy, and later facism, were primarily or even exclusively the concern of the Anglo-Saxon peoples and the peoples of Western Europe. But democracy by definition is a process of adjusting the demands and interests of all people by giving decision to the majority and at the same time protecting the basic rights of the minority. Democracy therefore has an inherent tendency to become a world order. The better it works, the more people it attracts, and this has in our time led to the decisive question: Is democracy to be expanded to take in those who do not yet have it, or is it to be restricted to those who already have it?

Now, for many, many decades we have been living in the most blissful fools' paradise, on the assumption that since we have the democracy we want, that is all that matters. But today we live in a world which, by reason of communications alone, let alone many other things, is a world in which isolation is physically impossible. The consequences of things done in any part of the world spread to all other parts of the world. The fact that we are a democracy has a tremendous impact on hundreds of millions of people who do not have democracy. If democracy is going to survive or if democracy is going to be extinguished in this world

we live in, it has got to be a question for the whole
world and nothing less than the whole world. The
fact is that more than half of the living human beings
in the world today do not have democracy; and the
democracy of the smaller half of living mankind cannot survive unless democracy is given to those who
do not have it and are already fit for it, and made available for others who do not have it as soon as they become fit for it.

The areas which Japan has penetrated or occupies
today can be put roughly into two categories. Using
an unfortunately inexact choice of words, we describe
all these areas as Japan's conquests. Now, the northeastern provinces of China, which we rather mislead-
ingly call Manchuria, and the other parts of occupied
China cannot properly be called "conquered" territory by anybody who has respect for the meaning of
words, because those areas have never resigned themselves to conquest and have never ceased to struggle
against conquest. Even Korea, occupied for decades
by Japan, cannot in any spiritual sense be called a conquered country. The only conquered countries are
certain of the colonial areas, and not all of these. The
Philippines, for instance, are not conquered. They are
an occupied country, but a country that is still fighting.

It is only those colonial areas which did not resist
or struggle, the areas where the people bowed their
heads to let the storm of Japan pass over, that can be
called conquered, because those were the areas where
the people did not have enough democracy to fight for
and not enough hope of democracy, self-rule, self-government, to fight for. Before this war is over it is going to become a major military question, whether these
countries are to be liberated from Japan with their
own participation in the struggle, or re-conquered
from Japan. We know that Korea, despite its long
subjection, is not a country that is going to be re-conquered from Japan. We know that it is going to be,
liberated from Japan, because the tradition of Korean
freedom has never died, and because there is in Korea
today, and on the fringes of Korea in the mountains
of the northeastern provinces of China, already a
nucleus of Koreans who have lived as guerrilla fighters
and are prepared to make any sacrifice to help free
their people.

These are questions that we must think about as
American citizens. The technical problems of military
operation, the co-ordination of the front lines and the
lines of supply, the timing together of military effort
on the land, on the sea and in the sky are not questions that you and I can decide, because we do not
have the specialized knowledge.

But there *are* questions that concern us very deeply. Are we, the people of America, making known to the people whom we elect to represent us in our government what kind of war we want to fight? Are we realizing that characteristic of democracy which I tried to describe a while ago: the fact that democracy must go ahead or must retreat? Because if we are fighting to bring the world back only to December 6, 1941, we are not fighting for democracy. We are fighting merely to push things back where they were and hope they won't deteriorate again as they did before, and that is no constructive way to win the kind of war we are in.

Only in proportion as we realize this characteristic of the world war as a whole, only as we realize that the war in the Pacific is not to be decided on questions of priority with the war in the west, but to be decided homogeneously with the war in the west, can we understand the importance of the fact that we are still not in the lead of the movement to make this a war to create democracy. In that respect we are still behind the Chinese, in spite of the fact that we already have what the textbooks call democracy and they don't yet have what the textbooks call democracy.

The questions of the peace are likely to be decided by the *way* in which the war is won much more than they are to be decided by whether the war is won first in Europe or first in China. And one thing that is encouraging, to me at least, is that I have talked to a good many people in the two countries which I know best. I don't want to exclude the Russians and the British and the Danes and the Free French and the Norwegians and the rest, but I can speak with more authority about America and China, and there the thing that encourages me is that when these problems are laid out to be discussed and thought about and debated, the essential reaction is the same, in both countries. In that similarity of response I see something much more important than the mechanical differences between our culture and that of China, and I see something which to me shows that we can not only win this war but win it in the right way and win it so that such a war will not have to be fought by our children twenty or twenty-five years from now.

PROBLEMS OF PEACE BEYOND
THE PACIFIC

II.

PROBLEMS OF PEACE BEYOND
THE PACIFIC

THERE is quite a widely held opinion in this country that the Japanese will be even more difficult to defeat than the Germans; that the Japanese will never collapse; that they will have to be killed off one by one all the way back to their homeland and a fight of extermination waged in the Japanese Islands. This I do not believe. It is one thing to concede the toughness of the Japanese as opponents. They *are* tough opponents. We shall have to fight, and fight very hard, to beat them. But they can be beaten and they can be beaten not step by step but in wholesale defeats.

There is one very pertinent piece of evidence which I think has been too much forgotten in this country because we have, so far, fought the Japanese, when we were attacking, in areas where they were pretty well cornered, like Guadalcanal and New Guinea, and where isolated Japanese who already had a feeling of desperation were told by their officers that if they tried to surrender they would suffer horrible mutilations and tortures. In such places they have fought with the desperation of cornered rats, as might have been expected. But this again shows the value of learning from our allies the things we still need to learn. One of the great strategic and psychological defeats of the Japanese army occurred when they took Nanking, advancing from Shanghai, at the end of 1937. The real story of the massacre, rape and loot at Nanking has never yet been told. The truth is far more horrible than anything that has yet been revealed in this country; but the real lesson of it has been missed.

This was the one time when the Japanese army had actually within its grasp the opportunity to surround and annihilate the cream of the Chinese army in a Tannenberg defeat. They failed because they ran amuck. These, remember, were crack troops of the Japanese army and yet they got completely out of hand; not only the men, but many of the officers. The remaining officers could not get them under control again. That is a really striking psychological index, of which we ought to make use.

One of the successful aspects of Japanese propaganda in this country has been the story of Japanese unity, discipline, dour, grim, unbreakable unity. That is a complete myth. When a victorious army built up of the most disciplined troops in Japan runs amuck like that, it proves that the Japanese are subject to mass hysteria. I think it is a common sense and reasonable inference that an army which is subject to mass hysteria when it is victorious and has an even greater victory in its grasp is an army that is also subject to mass hysteria and panic when it is defeated.

The thing that we have to remember is the difference between the battlefield of China and the battlefield of the Pacific Islands. If we were to commit ourselves to a march back to Japan island by island we should be fighting the Japanese in the way which makes them toughest. This gives a hopeful significance to the recent statement by General MacArthur that we are not bound to an island by island campaign, but have worked out a technique by which we can strike deep into the heart of the Japanese strength.

The battlefield on which the Japanese are most vulnerable is the Chinese battlefield, because there they are spread out over truly enormous distances and subject to the psychological hazards of doubt and fear and suspicion and distrust. That is the battlefield on which the rumor may spread through the Japanese army, once they have been pounded hard enough: "The men on our right are giving way. The men on our left are not to be depended on. We had better save ourselves." An army which behaved in victory as the Japanese did at Nanking is an army that at a psychological

moment like that will break and run and keep on running and never rally. If we fight this war rightly we
can count on very heavy fighting to begin with but a
rapid spurt to victory once we have broken the Japanese—and they can be broken. The Chinese have
proved that. However, whether the victory comes
soon or late, whether it proves hard or easy, we still
have to be conscious of the fact that the real problems of our generation are the problems of victory,
even more than the problems of war.

A major point to be considered here is one that has
already been raised: the beginning of final victory
may come in the west against Hitler; but the most
important consequences of victory may yet be the
consequences in Asia rather than the consequences in
Europe. We ought to stand back and examine, in good
time, ourselves and our prejudices, our pre-formed
opinions.

In spite of the interest that we may have in Asia, the
almost instinctive sympathy that we have for a country like China, especially here on the Pacific Coast, it
still remains true that our American cultural traditions,
our ways of thinking and acting and doing things,
trace back in a direct line to Europe, not to Asia. They
trace *forward* to Asia; but in a rather uncertain, grop-
ing way. If you search, in a time of war like this—as

the government searches and as every private institution searches—for experts on foreign affairs, people who know the languages and institutions and customs of other countries, you will immediately discover how many people there are who know, with some degree of authority, the problems of European countries— and how hard it is to find people who really know what's what in Asia. A natural result of that is that in our councils and deliberations, in the discussion that goes on before policy is determined, the preponderant weight is on Europe. We have a set bias toward Europe. Toward Asia we not only do not have that kind of bias, we have the handicap of a particular habit of thinking.

For a long time, and especially for the last one hundred years, we have thought of Asia as primarily an area in which we do things, an area in which we decide things for the people who live there. We are still not ready to appreciate the fact—and understand its consequences—that Asia in our time is an area in which decisive events can originate which determine our own course of conduct before we can determine it for ourselves. That is one of the major factors in the world of our time. The lesson is already there. It is already clear. It is up to us to appreciate it before it is too late.

In talking about the war itself I have laid the major emphasis on China because, in my belief, the course of the war as a whole, not only in the Far East but all over the world, was so largely predetermined by the way in which the Chinese fought in the years before the rest of us (with perhaps the exception of the Russians) understood that a world war had already begun. In the issues of the peace it is obviously not only China that counts. True, I think China is still perhaps the most important single area. There have been people who have spoken of the years to come after the war as the "American Century." Perhaps it is more likely that the next hundred years will be the Chinese Century.

Still, we ought not to make the mistake of swinging from one extreme to the other extreme. Important as China is, China is not the only factor in the post-war problem in Asia. On two sides of China there are two flanking problems of enormous magnitude, Russia and India. The moment an attempt is made to consider Russia and India, it becomes evident that the first thing that is needed is to clear the ground of an incredible mass of accumulated set habits of thinking, pre-formed opinions, prejudices, and facts which aren't so.

Let us take this from the point of view of the American Century. Let us take it from the point of view of a writer like Nicholas Spykman who has recently published a book called "America's Strategy in World Politics."

Spykman starts off with what seems to me the almost puerile assumption that immediately after this war our first job will be to revive Japan, in order to balance Russia and China. A more perfect booby trap for setting off the next world war I can't imagine. Then there are the people who say that we must grab naval and air bases all through the Pacific Ocean and on the coast of Asia, so as to see to it that America will be able to force all Asiatics, good and bad, to be good imitation Americans. Such thinking, even when expressed in terms of the next hundred years, shows an inability to get away from the obsessions of the past hundred years.

What are the facts? The facts are that for two hundred years, and especially for the last one hundred years, an enormously important area of the world, the Asiatic half of what the German geopoliticians call the "Eurasiatic land mass," the greatest continuous mass of land on the earth's surface, has been dominated, partly for geographical reasons and partly for technological reasons, by the nations which had sea power. The British sphere of influence from Suez eastward to India, the British Empire in India, the Dutch Empire in Netherlands India, the French Empire in Indo-China, the American sphere of economic and trading influence across the Pacific, were all built up on the fact that we acquired certain kinds of technology, characterized by great striking power, before the Asiatic peoples acquired them.

The reasons for which we acquired this priority in striking power are very interesting. They are one of the most fascinating chapters in history, but to go into them now would lead to a long digression from the main subject. Suffice it to say that, especially for the last hundred years, we have been able to dominate Asia by the "Gunboat Policy"—the ability to intimidate those Asiatic peoples who had not been conquered outright. This we shall never be able to do again.

As for Russia, I suppose the average American, when asked about the importance of Russia in Asia and in the Pacific, thinks of Vladivostok and Russia's supposed urge for warm water ports.

Now, the fact of the matter is that, both geographically and technologically, the age of the Gunboat Policy, and the naval control of the shores of Asia, has passed. Vladivostok itself, however essential to the Soviet structure within Siberia, is no longer to be considered as primarily the Russian gateway to empire in the Pacific. More important, for the next one hundred years, is the vast land frontier between Russia and China, from the Pacific to the Pamirs. A land frontier as open as that between Canada and the United States, and possibly even more important, it runs from Manchuria, (China's northeastern provinces) past Mongolia and Sinkiang or Chinese Turkistan, all the way to the Indian and Afghan frontiers in the deepest heart of Asia.

The things that will happen along that land frontier, far beyond the reach of any American gunboat or battleship, or airplane carrier or air base specified by the most ambitious American Centuryite, are of greater significance than anything that will happen in the Pacific Ocean.

In fact, the further west we go along that frontier, the further away from the sea we get, the more important the problems of the next hundred years are likely to be. The line of the frontier leads to the great highland masses of the Himalayas, the Karakorum, the Pamirs, and to what has long been known as the dead heart of Asia, the deep inland deserts of Chinese Central Asia and Russian Central Asia. This is the general area in which the frontiers of China, Russia, India, Afghanistan, Iran, either touch or approach each other. It is an area in which long-range railway hauls and long-range airplane flights will pay their maximum ton-mile dividends. It is an area which has lain dormant for many, many centuries, an area in which local, limited cultures of considerable brilliance have flourished in the past, but never flourished for long because there was no industrial complex to integrate together the varied resources and cultures of the grain-growing lands, the steppes, the mountains and the deserts.

With the penetration of the industrial technique into that part of Asia there will open up a vast and diversified area for the flowering of human society. There are untold resources in minerals—the greatest resources, perhaps, in all Eastern Asia except possibly for the area just between China, Burma and India at the other end of the Himalayas. There are enormous resources in hydroelectric power, and something else which Californians especially ought to be able to appreciate, one of the world's greatest reserves of unused land suitable for irrigated agriculture. What happens there in the heart of Asia will be something totally undreamed of by Admiral Mahan and all the other classic writers on naval strategy and oceanic routes.

If that is true, what of the future of China? And what of the future relations between China and Russia? Here we have to begin with the fact that the determining factors of the future of China do not lie on the coast, but in the deep western hinterland. It is the past of China that lies in the broad, flat eastern plains. The beginnings of industry were also planted, by foreigners, along the coast of China and the Yangtze River, where they could be protected by foreign gunboats and exploited under the security of foreign-imposed, unequal treaties, unequal laws, and special privileges. For this reason, the industry of China did not grow up as Pittsburgh and Chicago grew up. Pittsburgh and Chicago grew up functionally, because they suited the balance between sources of raw material, lines of communication and markets for the ultimate product. The early industries of China grew up for no such sound economic reasons; they grew up for political reasons because they could be protected and favored in particular spots.

That system was shattered by Japan's invasion of China. During 1937 and 1938 the Chinese succeeded in rescuing from Eastern China only a pathetic fraction of their industrial resources. What they did succeed in saving they moved to the far west, which had always been considered wild, undeveloped, crude, uncultured, barbaric by comparison with the rest of China. Once they had relocated their industrial plant, however, the Chinese found that it was the deep hinterland which in natural and functional ways most favored the growth of industry. This was where the raw materials and the hydroelectric power were most abundant, and where things could best be produced by a combination of technique and natural resources.

The China of the future, consequently, will not come back to the coast of China as the favored protegé of a victorious Britain and America. The main phenomenon will not be the "rescue" of China by Britain and America. The future of China will be firmly built in the heart of the country and from there it will expand back to the coast, bringing the coast under the control of the heart of the country. Never again will the heart of the country be dominated by foreign naval power or even foreign airplanes.

For the America of the next hundred years, access to Asia can hardly be considered apart from access to the Arctic. The greatest masses of the world's land surfaces are north of the Equator, which means that in order to fly from one major center of population and industry to another, most of the shortest and safest air routes pass either over or near the North Pole.

Now, the Arctic is an area in which the Russians and Canadians have been more enterprising pioneers than we ourselves. We, who pride ourselves so highly on our technological pre-eminence, must recognize that on this great frontier of the future we stand only in third place.

For the development of the Arctic as a whole we have a unique personal focus in the figure of Vilhjalmur Stefansson, whose career and work have influenced the American, the Canadian, and the Russian Arctic. In America, however, Stefansson is still popularly regarded as a romantic discoverer. In Canada, his work has contributed more directly to Arctic expansion; but it is in Russia, through the influence of Stefansson on Schmidt and other pioneers, that "Stefansson thinking" has had the most spectacular success, with the result that it is the Russians who are today the world's leaders in Arctic navigation, flying, and Arctic living.

In the future we shall be able to catch up with them. We still have a better over-all technology than they. However, the most important fact is that the Arctic is an area which is hardly to be conquered by us from the Russians or conquered from us by the Russians. The Arctic is an area in which, for the sake of all concerned, Americans, Canadians and Russians, will have to work out a complicated and very far-flung system of co-ordinated flying fields, weather stations and everything else that goes to the making of a modern network of airways and safe navigation.

Above all, we have to fit the question of the Arctic into a vast new pattern, another part of which is the importance of the inland frontiers of Asia—remembering that the direct route to the heart of Asia is to fly from the United States across the Arctic, rather than the Pacific.

This brings us to a question which worries many people, a question which I have tried to think out for myself as honestly and simply as I can; the question of the part to be played in the future by Russian propaganda and the spread or attempted spread of Bolshevism. This is, of course, a question which cannot be determined in terms of Asia alone. It is one of the questions that shows us that all problems of our time are world problems. If there is a question of subversive propaganda in Asia it cannot be considered apart from subversive propaganda in Eastern and Western Europe and in our own hemisphere.

Trying to work this out as a man who knows much more about Asia than he does about Western Europe or the southern part of the American Hemisphere, I have come on certain things which impressed me very much. I do not put them up to you as an authority, because I cannot pretend to be an authority. Perhaps I oversimplify the question; but comparing what I know about Asia with what I read about regions like the Balkans and Eastern Europe, two facts have struck me. First, there is the fact that after this war, if we are to have a peaceful and orderly development rather than a revolutionary development, we must have good government. Second, there is the fact that the decisive possibilities and responsibilities of good government today are not in the hands of leftists or revolutionaries. As far as I can make out, the peoples of Asia, of Europe, and of the Americas, all want such simple, normal human things as a home, a family, a job, a bit of private property, a bit of security for the future, a chance to give our children a better break than we have had. If we go on from this, we come to the fact that if there should be widespread subversion and revolution following the war it will not be the successful work of leftists and revolutionaries; it will be the result of the clumsiness and stupidity of the conservatives and the liberals who now have the situation in their hands. This seems to me to define a responsibility that lies directly on the present governments of America, Britain, and China.

Maybe I am oversimplifying things, but I think that if you will look back into history you will see that revolutions are not originated by successful revolutionaries. Revolutions are not produced by good propaganda. Revolutions are produced by bad government, and the outstanding example is the Russian revolution, which was not the work of the Bolsheviks. When the Tsarist Empire fell, it fell by the weight of its own incompetence and corruption. When the Tsarist Empire fell Lenin was in Switzerland, Stalin was in exile in Siberia, and almost every important Russian communist leader was either in prison, in Siberian exile, or abroad. It was not the Communists who destroyed the Tsarist Empire; the Tsarist Empire destroyed itself.

After the Tsarist Empire fell the Communists did not seize power; power devolved on Kerenski, a man who had an amazing talent for talking like nothing on earth and doing nothing on earth. It was only when he had further ruined the situation already ruined by the Tsarists that the Bolsheviks came into power— because millions and millions of people who had never wanted to be revolutionaries were forced to follow the revolutionaries after the people who stood for law and order and good government had proved themselves incapable of law and order and good government.

How much can we learn from yesterday? To-morrow in Yugoslavia, in Poland, in all the Balkan countries, in China, in Korea, in Japan, the deciding factor is in our hands. The power of decision is neither with Moscow gold nor with the golden tongues of Moscow. The power of decision rests on whether we make the mistake of assuming that strong government is more important than good government.

Perhaps the situation will be largely saved for us by the Chinese. Many people talk of the danger of civil war in China at the end of this war, but I think that the danger of civil war in China is probably less than the danger of civil war in many countries in Europe. One reason is that we have in Asia a world statesman, of real genius, in Chiang Kai-shek.

One of the oldest historical controversies turns on the question of whether great men create the events of their time, or are created by them. The career of Chiang Kai-shek shows that the problem cannot be limited to such narrow terms. The truth is that great men and great events interact on each other in a subtle and close way that results in creating history. This is as true of Roosevelt, Churchill, and Stalin as it is of Chiang Kai-shek. What may be called the functional test of the historical importance of Chiang Kai-shek is the fact that, throughout an already long political career, he has grown steadily greater and greater. The greater the crises through which he has led his people, the greater he has become as a symbol. The greater the decisions he has made, the greater the decisions he is able to make. In this he is a part of the contemporary history of all Asia. In China and India and the Philippines today the machinery for *selecting* representatives of the people is crude and inefficient. The leaders are to a large extent self-selected. Yet they are leaders, and the direction in which they are leading their peoples is democratic, because what gives a Chiang, a Gandhi, a Nehru, a Quezon his power over the minds of millions is his ability to make decisions and indicate courses of action which those millions will support and follow. Unless they continue to make such decisions, the people will not continue to follow them. There can be no doubt that this is a phase of creative energy leading to the emergence of true democracy out of the Asiatic societies. Already such peoples as the Koreans, the Indonesians, the Annamese, the Thais are at the verge of the same phase of development.

This is what draws, for the rest of us, the dividing line between the colonial phase of Asiatic history, which is now ending, and the phase of self-government, which is now beginning. Already, the major decisions are no longer up to us. The test of our political sagacity will not be in the decisions that we make, but in the skill and timing with which we accommodate ourselves to major decisions made in Asia by the peoples of Asia.

That brings us to India, in whose affairs any American must tread delicately. To discuss India without criticism is frankly unrealistic. What matters is the intent of the criticism. If it is criticism that diverts attention from things that deserve criticism in America, and centers on things that Americans do not like about the British Empire, it is destructive. If it is criticism that leads toward a common solution of problems which most Americans and most Englishmen want to see solved, it can be constructive.

We Americans ought to be aware that we slip easily and smugly into the habit of criticizing Britain, taking a holier-than-thou attitude about the British Empire. It is true that in the great years of modern empire building, especially in the 18th and 19th centuries, the major territorial acquisitions and the major colonial systems were set up by the British. While this is not a side issue, it is by no means the only issue. The deeper truth is that the growth of modern imperialism and the growth of the modern capitalistic system of free enterprise have been so closely intertwined from the beginning that they cannot be cut apart by any sharp formula of words.

If Americans have any real right to criticize the British, it is because we Americans are involved as deeply as the British in a world economic system in which cheap colonial labor, unprotected by the right to vote, is used to extract cheap raw materials to bring back to the factory areas of Britain and America, to be processed into cheap commodities by mass production methods and exported back to the colonial areas to be sold under the protection of colonial tariffs. We are not involved in quite the same ways as the British, but we are involved deeply enough so that we belong to the same system.

The "Open Door" principle, the principle of equality of opportunity which America has preached for so long, is in fact an American claim to share the benefits of British and Dutch and French empire all over the world while avoiding the responsibilities of political rule in the British and French and Dutch empires. We must therefore realize that when we criticize the colonial system we should feel ourselves bound, if not legally at least morally, to criticize ourselves.

This brings us to the major question. If we are fighting a war for democracy, then we must take Asia into account because it is only in a very limited part of the world, and only for a limited percentage of the world's population, that we are fighting to protect a democracy which already exists. East of Suez and west of Honolulu there lives more than one-half of mankind; four hundred fifty million in China, nearly four hundred million in India, seventy million in the Dutch East Indies, more millions in Malaya, in Burma, in Siam and Indo-China. Until the rise and emancipation of modern China, the overwhelming majority of these millions has not had the right to govern itself; has had so little right that even in India you can be imprisoned for subversive activity by merely stating in public that you want to rule yourself at some time in the future. If we are fighting for a world of elementary human freedom can we shut out half the world and call it a world system? If we do, we are fools. We have got to solve that problem. We cannot solve it simply by saying that Americans are better than others. We can only solve it by admitting and accepting our share of the responsibility for making things work better on a world scale.

The political problem is associated with yet another aspect of the world problem as a whole: the racial problem—the old, old prejudice which says that people whose skins are not white are only fit to be ruled by people whose skins are white; the old, old prejudice which says that if we give up our imperialism it will only be superseded by a colored imperialism. Americans can try on themselves one simple test: "What is the Yellow Peril, or any other colored peril?"

It is a supposititious, hypothetical peril, something which might happen in the future if our arbitrary color theories work out. How many people who talk about these potential perils realize that for two or three hundred years there has been only one real color peril—the White Peril which has been the most searing and brutal and pitiless factor in the lives of millions and millions of humanity?

There is one more thing that should be mentioned in even so brief a summary as this—the question of the future of Japan. Certainly the Japanese will be tough to beat; but they can be beaten; beaten completely, beaten to the point where they collapse. What shall we do then? I think that if we are to have a stable and enduring peace after the war we must stop short of any tendency to impose a permanent lynch-law subjection on Japan. We should consider, here, the patience and wisdom of the Chinese, who have suffered far more from the Japanese than we ever have, and who have never yet, after nearly six years of Japanese brutality, said that there must be a permanent punitive peace against Japan.

The power of the Japanese military must be absolutely shattered, and with the power of the military, the power of those great feudal families whose influence and control penetrate throughout the agricultural, the industrial, the urban and the rural life of Japan. When that has been done, however, we cannot impose on the Japanese a status which permanently subjects them to a lower level than other people, for this reason: That we cannot have a good peace unless we have an end to the colonial system. If we are putting an end to the colonial system elsewhere, or if we intend to set up at least a method by which peoples and nations can progress from colonial subjection to free self-government, then we cannot at the same time put the Japanese back into a colonial status. The two things would be so inconsistent that it would ruin the poise of the world as a whole. I am sure that this view is widely accepted in China, and I suspect that it would be accepted even in countries like Korea, which have suffered for years the impact of Japanese imperialism.

One of the greatest tests of our ability to shape the world, to show the power of mankind and the power of civilization over the brute material facts of the world will in fact be the obscure question of Korea. The question is not obscure in itself; it is obscure simply because Americans have paid so little attention to it. Korea is a country that stands at the corner between Russia and China and Japan; a country which has suffered longer under Japanese brutality than China's Northeastern Provinces or any other territory except Formosa seized by Japan; a country which will put to the crucial test our old, smug, complacent American attitude that Asia is a place which gets things done to it rather than a place in which things happen that matter.

Although there has been a certain amount of academic discussion of whether Korea should be free, it seems to me cold and bloodless and inhumane that so few people speaking and writing in America have realized the fact that in Korea there are more than twenty million people who are determined to be free because they know that being free is the only thing worth while.

Korea is a test case because it is a small country, a homogeneous country, a relatively isolated country. Unless we, in America, with our ideas of our great destiny, our great future, our great responsibility beyond the Pacific as well as on our own side of the Pacific, can learn to bring into focus at one and the same time our own problems and the problems of the great peoples, the powerful peoples, the rich peoples, and also the small but compact and deserving and heroic simple peoples of Asia; unless we show some ability to comprehend in one understanding, the far and the near, the great and the small, then if there is a third world war a large share of the blame will lie on us.

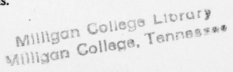

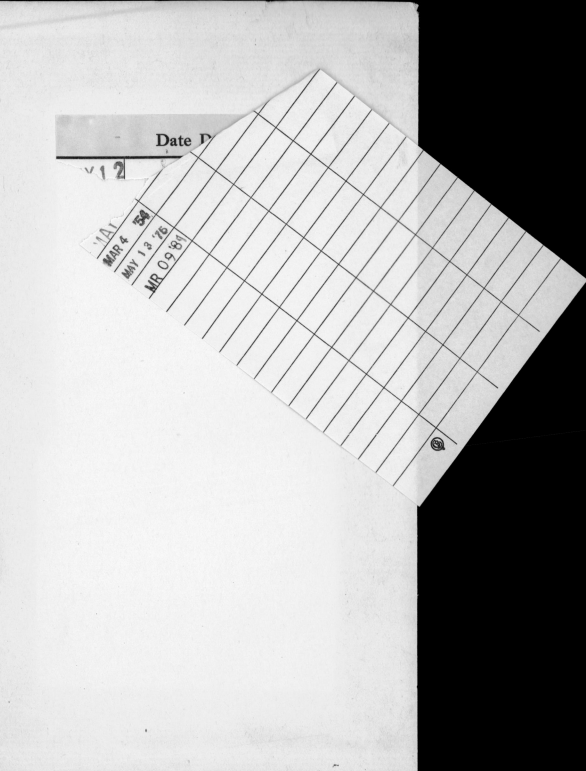